Early American Country Interiors

Early American Country Interiors

TIM TANNER

GIBBS SMITH
TO ENRICH AND INSPIRE HUMANKIND

To the Founding Fathers and all the many hands who, under God, forged this great nation of the United States of America. Your works still speak to those who have ears to hear. May we as citizens never forget your sacrifices for us, and never take for granted what you have handed to us. It is you whom I honor in these pages.

First Edition
17 16 15 14 13 5 4 3 2 1

Text © 2013 Tim Tanner
Photographs © 2013 Tim and Johnna Tanner, except photographs on pages 43, 44, 49, 53, 54, 55, 76, 108, 129 (left), 141, 150, and 151 © 2013 Brian Brown

Published by
Gibbs Smith
P.O. Box 667
Layton, Utah 84041

1.800.835.4993 orders
www.gibbs-smith.com

Cover and book design by Michelle Farinella Design
Printed and bound in Hong Kong

Gibbs Smith books are printed on either recycled, 100% post-consumer waste, FSC-certified papers or on paper produced from sustainable PEFC-certified forest/controlled wood source. Learn more at www.pefc.org.

Library of Congress Cataloging-in-Publication Data

Tanner, Tim.
  Early American country interiors / Tim Tanner. — First Edition.
    pages cm
  ISBN 978-1-4236-3276-4
1. Interior decoration—United States. 2. Decoration and ornament, Early American. 3. Decoration and ornament, Rustic—United States. I. Title.
  NK2003.T36 2013
  747.0973—dc23
                        2013003185

Acknowledgments

My sincerest thanks go out to the owners of these incredible homes. I have truly enjoyed seeing their creativity on display, and becoming fast friends with each of them. It is easy to see and feel their love for history and all things old. They are: David T. and Lora Smith (Ohio), Roger and Sylvia Libbey (Maine), Bill and Cheryl Bonin (Massachusetts), Lothar and Anita Janke (Utah), Sara Jense (Utah), Cody and Kari Wright (Utah), Bruce and Bonnie Barker (Utah), Larry and Sandy Neary (Connecticut), Tom and Mary Sayre (Kentucky), Paul and Toni Willmott (Ohio), Ben and Elaine Walden (Kentucky), Noah H. and Lynne Bradley (Virginia), Bill and Marise Craig (Virginia), Ryan and Ali Grubbs (Kentucky), Michael and Kathie O'Connor (Virginia), John and Geri Stukel (Idaho), Howard and Marsha Miller (Ohio), Rich and Jean Clinch (Illinois), Dan and Janet Edwards (Michigan), Steve and Devona Porter (Kentucky), Hank and Sally Spaulding (Kentucky), John and Jill Mahan (Kentucky), Dr. William and Amy Lewis (Kentucky), Lee and JoAnne Erdman (Ohio), Mark and Fredda Westfall (Ohio), Bill and Ginny Curry (Ohio), and Pat Linton (Ohio).

Special recognition goes to my friend Ginny Curry, who is the master of primitive style! And mountains of gratitude are not enough for David T. Smith. I tease David that I'm publishing another catalog for him—but the reality is that I so admire his work that just about everything he creates I want to photograph!

Brian Brown is also worthy of my appreciation. He and I took a trip several years ago to photograph some of these homes. I ended up with some of his incredible work and his great friendship.

Publisher Gibbs Smith and editor Bob Cooper cannot be thanked enough—for this opportunity and their patience with my abilities!

Finally, indescribable thanks goes to my wife, Johnna. Once again she has put up with my extra hours of traveling, photographing, and writing. She has been a tremendous support, taken many of the photographs, and loves this style as much as I do.

Thank you all!
—Tim Tanner

Contents

Foreword

In the fall of 1988 I was sitting in an illustration class at Utah State University. The professor, Glen Edwards, had just finished critiquing our weekly paintings. I don't recall how it went for me but I do remember what happened next. A tall, slender "new guy" came through the door into our class. He seemed somewhat familiar to me. (I think Tim Tanner seems familiar to most people, even though they don't know him.) He talked with the professor and then dug from a bag some paintings he had brought with him. We as students were anxious to see what the new competition had to offer.

Tim's paintings were very different than what we were doing in this particular class. The paintings were portraits of different characters but were highly designed, in fact the design seemed to be the most important part of each piece. Don't get me wrong, the paintings were great, but the design was fantastic.

Over the many years that I have known Tim a lot of things have changed. We have followed each other back and forth across the country as friends, neighbors, and colleagues. We have modeled for each other for our various illustration projects, fished together, hunted together, camped with our families together, and on occasion sorrowed together. Tim and his family are as familiar to me and mine as, well, family.

I have watched with curiosity, and I have to admit with some envy, how Tim has always designed not only his paintings and other artistic endeavors but the spaces around him to look and feel the way he sees the world, with the simplistic beauty of days gone by. He designs every facet of his surroundings, whether it is the way he is dressed or his latest building project. It could be a simple chicken coop or the renovation on a potentially "great old house," but he sees things differently than most of us do, and he makes sure that the design remains fantastic.

In Tim's world everything is placed in the right place. He follows intuitively the rules and principles that are important to design and composition. Proper symmetry is achieved here and there, correct spacing of the elements involved, the shape and lines seem to effortlessly fall into place, the colors of each object are complementary to their surroundings or create the focal point that he wants to achieve, the paint has to be applied in a specific way to accomplish the "right feel," and on and on. Just writing this makes my head spin with options. I often refer to Tim as a Renaissance man. He can do a lot of things—he's a designer, painter, musician, builder, historian, maker of many things interesting—but probably at the top of his list would be husband and father.

I look forward to seeing what Tim is up to next. Whatever it is I'm sure it will be beautifully designed and very pleasing to the eye. He will give us another glimpse into his world, and I'm sure it will cause me to think that I should be more conscientious of design not only in my world but also in my next painting.

—Dan Burr
Tetonia, Idaho
March 24, 2013

Introduction

Have you ever walked into a retail shop and heard music playing? It's an occurrence that most of us are very familiar with. Imagine spending an entire day shopping, and every store you go into is playing the same song. In each shop you enter, the same notes are heard. At the start of the day the song is new and refreshing—a cheerful bit of music, pleasant to the ears. But as your shopping day progresses it becomes increasingly tiring. Thankfully there are a few slight variations. In some shops the chorus is playing; in others a verse. At times the arrangement is slightly slower, in other locations it's more upbeat. Some shops even have an arrangement with more or less instruments. But regardless of the arrangements, it is nevertheless the same song. By the time you are done shopping you're to the point that if you heard it once again on the final day of your life, that would be one day too soon. That catchy, upbeat tune that sounded so energizing first thing in the morning now pounds on your brain and makes you want to scream.

This is similar to the way we respond to the latest, greatest styles in today's technologically advanced society, where we are all eager to follow the current crazes. They might be the latest fashion trends, the most politically correct health diet, or the most popular reality TV show.

This phenomenon of everyone craving the latest style is especially apparent in our modern homes. One can drive through a twenty-first-century subdivision and see the evidence. Every house looks basically the same—with only very slight differences. The colors change slightly, the windows are configured a little bit differently, the stucco is on the right side on one house and on the left side next door. One can pretty well guess what's behind the walls. The latest wall colors, the newest high-tech appliances, the trendiest cabinets and countertops.

Don't get me wrong. Repetition is a good thing—even very desirable, as we'll discuss later in this book. Housing developments that conform to limited and similar treatments are actually models of an effective design principle. Cohesiveness in the look and feel of a group of items is appealing to the human eye.

But perhaps the largest problem with the "latest greatest" syndrome is that society is fickle. Sure, something may be the cat's meow today. But by its very nature, that pretty well guarantees it won't be the cat's meow tomorrow (see, even *phrases* become outdated). Just like the song in the opening analogy, the latest styles start out new and refreshing. But with time they can become nearly unbearable. Just around the corner from that ultramodern subdivision is an out-of-style 10-year-old development, and beyond that sits one that is 20 years old and definitely showing its age. And then there's that group of houses across town that are so dated that no one with the least bit of fashion savvy would be caught dead living in one of them!

So how have we learned to deal with changing fashions? There have been three basic responses throughout history. First, if one has a never-ending bank account and can just switch houses every 10 years or so, updating to the latest crazes, one can just eschew the population of ne'er-do-wells and rise above them. Sounds rather ridiculous, doesn't it? Yet it's surprisingly the avenue that many people aspire to. Most don't quite pull it off because of that never-ending bank account thing, but wish they could, and worse, become depressed when they can't. Some young people get themselves into trouble, teetering near the precipice of financial ruin trying to accumulate what it took Dad and Mom 30 years to amass. In fact, many of them have what Dad and Mom never managed to assemble, living life as if being out of fashion were against the law.

The second response has been to simply not be concerned about home fashion sense. Some folks are just blessed, perhaps, by a black hole when it comes to visual awareness— the architectural equivalent of guys who get that look from their spouses that says, "You're not actually going to wear those socks with that shirt in public, are you?" On the surface, this response appears much saner than the first, and perhaps it is. But it has one big fallacy: we're all born with an inherent appreciation and desire for visual fulfillment.

Even prehistoric peoples created art on their cave walls.

Which brings us to response number three, which, based on thousands of years of examples to back up my hypothesis, I propose might be the wisest: first of all, *consciously choose to be different*; then *choose a style that exhibits time-proven, universal principles of design* that will make any object visually appealing; and finally and perhaps most importantly, *choose the warm, familiar atmosphere that the word "home" embodies.*

One could just choose something different—but contrary to some modern art movements, difference alone does not necessarily equate to visual appeal. Similarly, one could use proven design principles while choosing something different and also achieve success—this is the essence of modern style. The design principles that we'll later discuss in detail work just as well with modern architectural design as they do with historical design. If modern style is your preference, you are in good company and it's not my intention to persuade you otherwise. But for many of us, a house isn't really a home without the familiarity aspect. For us, what we all crave deeply is not a visual sense of fashion, but a visual sense of warmth, comfort, familiarity, shelter, and peace. What we all really want is a *home.*

What you see in this book will probably be different than what you see in most homes today. In order to create a haven and refuge from the messiness of our daily existence, we often need a change of scenery—something that is obviously different. You can read a bit more about escaping the modern world with warm, cozy, historical surroundings in my first book, *Early American Country Homes: A Return to Simpler Living.* The focus of *this* book concerns combining design principles with the same kinds of wonderful, old, familiar objects and materials presented in that previous book. These time-proven design principles work apart from the latest trends and current must-haves. Something that is well designed will stand the test of time. It will be just as visually appealing 200 years from now as it is today.

I cannot fully describe Early American country style without simultaneously explaining principles of design; the two go hand in hand. You will probably find many of these principles familiar, having seen them used effectively all of your life. But explaining them will help you *know* that your designs are effective, rather than just having a hunch that they might be.

The principles of effective design have been known for centuries. They are evident in nearly every culture and every historical period. The ancient Greeks certainly had many of the visual design principles figured out. When Rome was conquering the world, subjugated countries were forced to assimilate Roman culture. Yet when Rome conquered Greece, the defeated Greeks had more effect on Roman culture than vice versa. Romans borrowed many aspects of Greek design in their visual objects and architecture. These universal principles are also found in other cultures and time periods, from ancient Egypt to aboriginal America, from thousand-year-old Chinese architecture to hundred-year-old Scandinavian furniture.

Long-forgotten principles of effective design from the classical worlds of Rome and ancient Greece were rediscovered during the Renaissance. The Renaissance in turn gave birth to the Age of Enlightenment, which would last for most of the eighteenth century. This age spawned the ideas and circumstances that would bring the United States into being. Along with the concepts of self-governance, religious tolerance, and individual freedom came enlightened ideas in science, mathematics, music, and art. "Renaissance men" such as Thomas Jefferson had an unquenchable thirst for all knowledge, whether it was political, botanical, or architectural. Those creating the buildings and furnishings of the era utilized those rediscovered principles of design. Jefferson's Monticello is an excellent example of the use of classic design principles. Colonial styles and influences continued into the early nineteenth century in the United States. Even in the buildings of a farmer in Maine or a frontier Kentucky backwoodsman, one could find the use of design principles that originated in ancient Greece. While those early settlers may not have been aware of it, their backwoods cabins shared design principles with the Parthenon.

One of the main reasons that many of us are enamored with Early American style is that it combines the use of design principles with a casualness that is warm and homey. While much of our time has to be spent in the outside world at work, shopping, or in general societal interactions, listening to that same high-stress pounding song that the world can't get enough of, Early American style allows us to escape to quiet and peace. It is visually appealing and emotionally inviting because it is a marked difference from the rest of the world. It evokes the kinds of feelings and comments like that of a visitor to Bill and Marise Craig's wonderfully restored home in the Virginia countryside: "This home just wraps its arms around you!" Or the comment by Larry Neary from Connecticut, who described the restoration of his and wife Sandy's old colonial cape as "like finding an old pair of comfortable slippers that you forgot you had." To be honest, the principles of good design work with any type of architecture—ancient Egyptian to postmodern mid-twentieth century. But to many of us, while the principles may work in those other styles, they do not necessarily feel as much like home. Early American country style allows us to cast off the whole notion of having to have the latest, greatest fad. That 30-year-old dated home eventually comes back into fashion after several more decades, and, if one is aware of and uses time-proven principles of good design, never goes out of style again. Early American country style is certainly not for everyone (which is fortunate, since we don't want it to become the latest trend!), but for those whom it *does* speak to, it speaks volumes about coziness and hominess.

Good design is good design, regardless of how much the materials cost. Too many people think that good design equates to expensive granite countertops and state-of-the-art appliances—that it's measured by how much everything costs. Don't get me wrong, quality craftsmanship and materials will always be valuable. You will see the occasional granite countertop or expensive antique in this book. In these cases, the material or artifact *adds* to the effective design rather than *makes* it. You will see in our journey, however, that expensive materials are not the secret ingredient to beautiful spaces and cozy surroundings. In fact, free old galvanized tin is not only friendlier to the wallet than a more expensive material, but its use may occasionally even constitute better design.

So let's embark on this journey that significantly detours from that same latest trendy song playing everywhere else, and may you enjoy it!

Living Rooms and Keeping Rooms

Living and keeping rooms in the Early American home are often the epitome of comfortable living spaces. These rooms, if designed well, embody the ideals spoken of throughout this book. They are warm, inviting, and often display some of the most notable visual treats for the eye, including historical art and artifacts. Here one may escape the hustle and bustle of modern living more fully, surrounded by treasures and stories of bygone years. Living and keeping rooms also potentially offer a wider available palette of historical materials, textures, colors, and furnishings than other spaces in the home, allowing the perfect blend of focal points, repetition with variation, and harmony (some of the principles of design highlighted throughout this book).

I've also seen living and keeping rooms that perfectly blend modern technologies, with cozy in-floor heating, large-screen entertainment centers hidden imaginatively behind vintage doors, and dramatic, artistic lighting never dreamed of by our ancestors. For these reasons, living and keeping rooms can be some of the most enjoyable spaces to create in the Early American home.

What, you may ask, is the difference between a living and a keeping room? It's whatever you want it to be. In today's world, these spaces are most often referred to as living rooms (or great rooms when combined with dining and/or kitchen spaces). "Keeping room" is a term from yesteryear describing a similar space—not as formal as the parlor, and often the setting for warm, familiar gatherings. Because we are designing Early American spaces, many homeowners prefer to use the historical moniker "keeping room."

Many people enjoy collecting antiques and displaying their finds throughout their homes, like these wonderful pieces from the Clinch Home in Illinois.

Where does one start when decorating this delightful space? That partly depends on how set in stone the space is—whether one is dealing with a historical home with an already defined keeping room, a vintage home being remodeled, or a new home re-created to capture the charm of early America. But in any of the cases above, focal points are the most logical and wisest place to start. Does the keeping room have a hearth? If so, that's usually the most obvious area for a focal point. If not, is there a set of windows with a splendid view of the surroundings? What may not be a splendid view now can often be changed into one with a bit of exterior landscaping. Also note that a view doesn't necessarily have to be dramatic—sometimes a simple, friendly neighborhood or an old barn invokes feelings of contentment with one's setting. Blessed is the homeowner who has both a hearth and a pleasant view, for then one can choose both a primary and secondary focal point.

Even with no immediately evident focal points to work with, a wise decorator will establish areas of emphasis and areas that are subordinated. A couch with notable artwork hanging above it can become an engaging focal point. Don't be afraid to be creative with your focal point. I have found that when I am presented with a significant design dilemma, the stewing and fermenting while thinking of a solution often yields the most creative results.

One of the things I enjoy most about historical homes is their quirkiness. I've seen spaces that seemed to be insurmountable quandaries transition into favorite rooms. New construction often does not force this type of creativity, so often doesn't display the wonderful results. Whatever you determine your focal point to be, I would suggest the avoidance of the modern curse to excellent home design—the television. I'm not suggesting you go without; just recommending that you avoid the pitfall so common to the homes of today, in which the TV inadvertently becomes the main focal point of the living room (as an aside, some of my favorite examples of reproduction cabinetry have been fashioned to hide the TV).

After determining the focal point, incorporate the other principles of design presented in this book to fill out your room. I find my designs to be especially effective when I approach a space with the principle in mind first and the components second. For example, rather than wondering where I should place a chair that I happen to have, I ask myself, "In order to achieve a perfect example of repetition with variation, what items do I have that I could use, or for what should I be on the lookout to add to what I have?" Effective interior decorating is the perfect blend of practical positioning of furnishings with the stunning use of visual principles of design.

As far as a correct level of comfort, you are the one who gets to determine exactly where you want to be in the wide spectrum available to you. I have seen homes that are the epitome of period authenticity. I have seen others where a comfortable couch and a big-screen TV were of utmost importance. There are, in our day and age, manufacturers of reproduction furniture that are able to effectively accomplish both.

Rich and Jean Clinch created a modern-size family room space that is imbued with Early American charm. Nothing says that new construction has to appear new!

Right: The Barker Home in Sanpete County, Utah, displays numerous antiques from early Mormon history as well as an incredible collection of quilts that Bonnie has gathered over the years.

The images on these two pages are from John and Jill Mahan's beautiful new home in Kentucky. This house is a perfect example of a very modern home replete with Early American decor to give it personality that many new homes lack.

One of the main reasons that Early American articles
and furnishings are so appealing is that they exhibit
a delightful variety of textures, colors, and shapes.

The folk art painting on this living
room wall commemorates a local event
from the hills of West Virginia.

Right: Lora Smith is masterful at arranging the
Early American objects, old and new, in her and
David T. Smith's magical home in Ohio. David's
incredible skills as a craftsman and Lora's wonderful
talents are a combination that is tough to beat!

Lovely "smalls"—smaller antique or reproduction
objects—create a wonderful atmosphere and
visual treats in the Early American home.

Redware was a common item in the late eighteenth
and early nineteenth centuries. It is one of my favorite
items to decorate with because of the splashes of color.

Sally Spaulding's
home in Kentucky
was built in the late
1800s, but Sally
has artfully (and
masterfully, I might
add!) decorated
it with objects and
furnishings from
the eighteenth and
nineteenth centuries.

Early American style has many varieties, as these two still lifes
present. Both are in Kentucky, but one embodies primitive
style while the other celebrates a Thoroughbred farm.

While some homeowners choose a specific period
of history and stick to it, Early American style
lends itself well to an eclectic mix of periods.

What could be more inviting than this cozy family room? For those of you who are aghast at the lack of a television in the room—there is a big-screen TV behind the doors of that cabinet in the corner.

REPETITION *with* VARIATION

Two of the easiest principles of design to understand, and to successfully apply, are *repetition* and *variation*. In visual art, *repetition* essentially means adding more of a particular item. *Variation* means changing something about that item from one example to another. Some designers consider the two to be separate design principles, while others would argue that the two go hand in hand. Too much of either principle by itself will actually be counterproductive, so using one of these principles alone isn't as effective as using both in concert. Too much repetition equals boredom. Too much variety yields confusion. The secret, then, is to aim for the perfect amount of each—the "sweet spot" that lies somewhere between too much repetition and too much variation.

In the context of design, almost every thing can be improved by the repetition of that thing. Repetition automatically unifies a visual composition. Even an object that is relatively unexciting by itself can become remarkable in concert with others of its own kind. One single old bottle or flowerpot may be hardly noticed alone, but a collection of them becomes a visual treat. A relatively mundane item like a jar of preserves by itself is just something to eat. Add that jar of preserves to 50 others and stack them on a pantry shelf and they approach a work of art. I say "thing" above because this principle applies to more than just objects. Colors can be repeated, materials can be repeated, textures can be repeated—any kind of treatment can be repeated.

For example, a palette of colors can unify an entire house. For several years we've used in our homes a palette of Early American colors consisting of a warm antique white, colonial red, a dark olive green, a somewhat caramel-colored mustard, and lamp black, in addition to the natural wood. Just about every door, window, trim, and furnishing has been painted in these colors, or left as the natural wood color. Using this very limited palette pleasantly unifies the whole home. Variations occur with occasional antique pieces that don't follow the palette and the fact that each room displays the palette a bit differently. In the kitchen, the cabinets might be red, the window trim mustard, and a step-back cupboard black. In the living or keeping room, one could see green window trim, a black and mustard checkered fabric on the chairs, and a red cupboard hiding the television set. Variation is relatively easy to add when needed: a blue pantry box or wooden bucket, a multicolored old quilt over the back of a chair, or an antique sign in colors other than those in the limited palette.

Another example might be drywall, a building material that often borders on too much repetition, but is definitely an effective unifying element. The key is to add other elements to provide the necessary variety, and then to repeat those elements until they feel like just the right amount. An occasional wooden, painted wall is a welcome relief, but needs to occur in more than one location. Hand-hewn, weathered barn beams are a material that always enhances Early American-styled interiors. One of my favorite repetition-with-variation combinations is that of hewn-log walls in part of the home and a hewn-timber frame in another part. Stone and brick are always appropriate building materials. The trick is to use them in more than one place. One of the best examples of repetition is a stone foundation and chimney outside and the same stone on the fireplace inside. This unifies the exterior of the home with the interior. Obviously I'm not describing anything revolutionary or new. Old homes abound with the types of repetition and variation that I describe. That's the point—Early American homes are often a model of effective use of design principles.

Anything can be repeated. The angled braces in a timber-framed structure are repetitions of shape. A variety of baskets hanging from the ceiling become a repetition of texture. The use of old quilts on every bed is an example of a repetition of treatment. The point is to find that sweet spot between repetition and variation. Exactly how much repetition and how much variation to shoot for can be a bit tricky. Usually it's not a fifty-fifty proposition; I usually start with the repetition part of the equation being about 70 to 80 percent, with the variation around 20 to 30 percent—figures that may need adjusting.

A specific type of variation is based on changing the size of objects. A close artist friend refers to it simply as "big, medium, small." I use this principle often. For example, given the challenge of placing items above a fireplace mantle, I immediately begin looking for a large object, a medium-sized object or two, and several small objects. The large object may be a painting. Medium-sized objects might include a basket, a couple of redware plates, or an old hunting decoy. Small objects may consist of candlesticks or a few pinecones. The objects themselves are actually less important than their sizes. If an object fits within the parameters of the desired genre (in this case, Early American), and it's the right size in relationship to the other chosen objects, it will work.

The same idea works in other scales. In a room, a large TV cabinet, a medium-sized chair, and a small end table may be the chosen objects. In a landscape, a large barn, a medium-sized house, and a small woodshed might provide the necessary components. It is a simple but effective principle to keep in mind. Give it a try!

Kitchens

Kitchens are one of my favorite spaces in Early American homes. They can exude an incredible historical atmosphere. They are also one of the most challenging rooms in a vintage home. That's because, for the most part, the kitchens in actual Early American homes weren't at all like kitchens nowadays. Sure, there were a few similarities—food preparation is food preparation, after all. But when we envision a modern kitchen, we usually start out with cabinetry (all matching, of course); then a multitude of appliances large and small, such as the refrigerator, stovetop, oven, microwave, dishwasher, coffeemaker, toaster and mixer; add perhaps a kitchen island and the proverbial kitchen sink, and you have a modern kitchen.

When our pioneer forefathers (and mothers) envisioned a kitchen they had a completely different vision. Their kitchens centered around the cooking hearth, or later the wood cookstove. They also might have included a cupboard or two to store basic ingredients and spices (the cupboards seldom matched, if they were fortunate enough to have multiples); a simple scrubbed pine table for everything from kneading dough to cleaning fowl; a few open shelves to store a meager collection of plates or bowls (often not both); a drawer or two for knives, spoons, and forks; and, if the housewife was extremely fortunate,

a stone sink along one exterior wall. (Running water was dependent on whether whoever was carrying the water from the well or spring felt like walking . . . or *running*.)

So how do we deal with these two seemingly opposite approaches in designing an Early American country kitchen? We get to combine the best of the old with the best of the new, picking and choosing what we like about each. Why not, for example, add a fireplace to the kitchen area—or an old wood-burning cookstove? A "mismatched" set of cabinets in different (albeit still harmonious) styles and colors gives an excellent vintage look. Open shelves are great for displaying period-style bowls or plates. Treenware (wooden bowls and plates) looks especially great in a kitchen.

Try to think outside of the box. One of my favorite countertop treatments, for example, came from a fortunate surprise discovery. One of our old homes that my wife, Johnna, and I restored happened to have one layer of old, flat, galvanized tin as one of the seven layers of roofing that we had to remove when we reroofed. The antique patina on it was great! We used it on several kitchen and bathroom countertops over several years, and I was sad when we used the last of it. (One can use new galvanized sheets of tin and help advance the patina with some watered-down muriatic [hydrochloric] acid. Experiment with the solution first. And the fumes are toxic, so treat the metal before you take it inside.)

I have seen kitchens that have the incredible appearance of being over 200 years old, yet include state-of-the-art modern conveniences. Those that I am most familiar with are the work of David T. Smith. Those who are familiar with my books know that David is my hero when it comes to designing kitchens. For this reason, it seemed more appropriate to get his input for this chapter, as he is much more knowledgeable about kitchens than I am. Following are a few great ideas that he was kind enough to share.

Kitchen Design for the Historical Home

- With special attention to period architecture and the personal character of your home, blend the old with the new so your twenty-first-century kitchen fits into your Early American–style home.

- Define the available space for your kitchen. In the long run it may be worth it to increase the footprint by reconfiguring space or adding on. If you are knocking out walls, you may need an architect or engineer to tell you what is possible.

- Decide on a design style. Consider the age of your home (or the age that you want to convey) to help you determine styling of cabinets, etc. Get ideas from magazines or other sources. Sketch your space with exact measurements.

- Have a professional help you design and draw your space to scale. A professional deals with this every day and will have valuable knowledge that is well worth this planning effort. Try to find a designer/builder that is interested in history and understands what you are trying to achieve.

- Make sure that the design of your kitchen functions well and also fits with the character of your house. There are computer drawing programs that can show your kitchen design to scale and in 3-D. It is very helpful to see your kitchen in this way.

- Will your kitchen be a collected kitchen (multiple cabinet styles and colors) or a monochromatic kitchen? Does your home have architectural elements that can be incorporated into the design of your kitchen?

- Establish a budget. Here are some of the things to consider: architectural fees for structural work; demolition and site preparation; new lighting and electrical; flooring; cabinets and installation; appliances; countertops. Plan on going over your budget.

- Choose appropriate appliances, a sink, faucets, and countertops. You can achieve a more period look using appliances with panels and/or appliances behind doors. Soapstone, copper, or white apron sinks with matte-finished brass or copper faucets are appropriate in vintage homes. Countertops can be of wood, soapstone, or granite.

- Find a local contractor who is capable and is willing to work with you. Budget enough time to complete your project. Remember, if you do it right your new kitchen may outlive you. The designs that we are talking about are timeless. Don't get in a rush— you are preparing for decades of use. If you plan on selling your house, try to design a kitchen that will make you happy now and add value to your house later when you decide to sell.

- Don't design a custom high-end kitchen to look like a low-end mainstream kitchen, with overlaid doors, shiny white or cherry cabinets, Formica or composite countertops, cheap hardware, and existing old or low-end appliances.

- Doing a project like this can be costly and stressful, but it can also be very fulfilling and a lot of fun. Relax, plan well, save your money, find good people to work with, and have some fun.

You can by now, perhaps, spot
the extraordinary work of
David T. Smith in this creative
cabinetry surrounding the range
and the blue kitchen island.

Right: Ginny Curry's "collected
kitchen" comprises almost
entirely antique pieces housing
every modern convenience.

Left: This Early American home in Louisville, Kentucky, has an old fireplace in the kitchen. Note the brass bucket sunk into the island counter—plumbed as an extra sink.

The kitchen in this Ohio home is the brainchild of JoAnne Erdman and David T. Smith. A built-in oven hides under the opposite side of the island, and a dishwasher is hidden behind the panel to the left of the sink.

For those who prefer a less-primitive style, here's
a great example from Noah H. Bradley III—a
modern kitchen with Early American accents.

A stunning kitchen in this Michigan home. Owners Dan and Janet Edwards collaborated with David T. Smith on the unusual treatment above the range—inspired by old fireplace mantles.

Note the refrigerator behind the cream-colored cabinet panels in this kitchen in a home near Lexington, Kentucky.

Right: Many colonial taverns had cage bars, such as this wonderful example. The original is in a tavern in Massachusetts. This reproduction is in a Connecticut home.

Variations of colonial red
always brighten up a kitchen,
imbue an Early American
atmosphere, and liven up the
space, as in these two kitchens
from homes in upstate
New York and Maine.

In the Libbey home in Maine, an antique table and
chairs form a small eat-in area, for use when the dining
room is too formal. A breadboard on the counter hides
the cooktop, and the two doors below hide the oven.

Historical colors are so important to create the Early American atmosphere. If to your eyes a variety of mismatched colors seems too stark compared to our modern mind-set of matching cabinets, here's an excellent example of color use in the kitchen of an Ohio home—where the cabinets do match.

Early American–styled kitchens are wonderfully
warm and cheerful, with variations of colors and
textures not usually seen in most modern kitchens.

An abundance of charm—and an abundance of food—
are usually found in the Early American kitchen.

Right: One can choose what to hide and what to show.
In this mid-nineteenth-century kitchen in a central
Utah home, a microwave happens to fit in well with
the china collection and handmade porcelain knobs.

Two views of the beautiful kitchen of John and
Jill Mahan, in their home in the bluegrass area
of Kentucky. Notice the stunning mix of painted,
granite, and natural curly maple surfaces.

One of the best things about building a modern home
with Early American furnishings is that dramatic
lighting can be utilized to enhance the setting.

The beautiful kitchen shown in both of these photos is from the Tucker House in Louisville, Kentucky—a wonderfully restored bed-and-breakfast. Owners Steve and Devona Porter have meticulously re-created an 1840s atmosphere throughout the entire home.

EMPHASIS, SUBORDINATION, *and* FOCAL POINTS

Imagine all the notes of a favorite song played all at once. What you normally enjoy would become nothing more than a loud, repugnant noise. Musical composers have a very significant tool at their disposal: *time*. They can present their compositions as fast or slow, moving or halting. The aspect of time is indeed one of the most important and critical factors in a musical composition. Designers, as *visual* composers, do not have this benefit of time. How long does it take to look at a room? The entire composition can be seen in less than a second. How does the designer avoid the visual equivalent of a loud, repugnant noise? The secret is to set up the composition so that the viewer sees it in separate pieces. We create a *visual hierarchy* by telling the viewer, "First I want you to look at A, next I want you to look at B, then I want you to look at C." By doing this we don't dump the entire composition onto the viewer at once; instead we hand it to them one bite at a time.

How do we create this visual hierarchy? The first step is to determine the hierarchy itself. What I want the viewer to look at first is commonly called the *main focal point*. Often in interior design a focal point is a grouping of things rather than an individual item. For example, the main focal point in a living or great room may be (and often is) the fireplace, including all of the things on or around it. That is one of the major reasons why I seldom design a home without a hearth. (The other big reason is that a hearth says "home" like few other things). After the main focal point, there are *subordinate focal points*. A good designer will determine the hierarchy of subordinate focal points in order, beginning with focal point number two—perhaps a particular setting of furniture, or a certain grouping of photos on the wall.

What is emphasized and what is subordinated, and where an item or group of items falls in the hierarchy, is not as important as the fact that the hierarchy exists. If you choose to have a painting be the main focal point and the fireplace a secondary, subordinate focal point, that is completely fine. Our main goal is to avoid unloading all visual information at once. In creating a visual hierarchy, the main thing to keep in mind is that the scheme needs to make sense to the viewer. It is possible, for example, using the principles of emphasis and subordination to have some obscure item that makes absolutely no sense be the main focal point. A brightly colored basket could easily grab the eye over anything else in a room, for example, if the rest of the room were colored in predominantly neutral tones. Generally speaking, our minds don't apply as much importance to something like a basket compared to something as substantial as a fireplace. So the hierarchy has to make at least a little bit of sense. One of the most common mistakes that amateur designers make is creating an accidental focal point as described.

How do we "tell" the viewer's eye what to look at first, then second, then third? Fortunately there is a universal language that every human being is hardwired with the capability to understand. Following are a handful of tools that can help you determine the proper emphasis and subordination hierarchy for your space:

VALUE CONTRAST. Artists and designers use the word "value" to describe the spectrum from dark to light. Picture black on one end, white on the opposite end, and a progression of grays in between.

This is called a value scale. The highest *value contrast* is black against white. High contrast really pops to the viewer's eyes. Lower-value contrasts are found in closer neighbors on the scale, and command less attention. Value contrast is more often than not the strongest tool in the toolbox. For example, if you have a black-and-white checkered floor, you have a very commanding focal point, one that would be quite difficult to override with anything else. Even though you may want the focal point to be something like the fireplace, the first thing everyone sees is that floor. A simple solution may be to paint the checkered floor in black and a relatively dark tan, or a similar low-contrast combination.

SIZE. As you can imagine, the *size* of an object affects its importance in the hierarchy. Large things usually command more attention than small things. But size is not as important as value contrast. One could have a huge painting on the wall, and if all the colors and values in the painting blend in with the wall, a relatively small item that displays high-value contrast—say a black-and-white vase—could easily command more attention than the painting.

PLACEMENT. Generally speaking, when an object is in the center of the composition it commands more attention than if placed at the edge. A cherished piece of redware, if given center stage on the mantle, will pop more than if that same piece were over in the far corner on a bookshelf. Its *placement* in the setting subliminally indicates its importance to the viewer.

LIGHTING. An object in *direct light* will usually command more attention than that same object in a darkened area.

CONTEXT. When an item is *different* than everything around it, it draws attention. This may be subtle, like a round table in a room where everything else is angular, or it may be quite stark, like a hot pink lava lamp sitting in an otherwise completely colonial setting (not recommended, by the way). The differences can be of any sort: shape, texture, historical period, value, color, etc.

COLOR TEMPERATURE. Most of us are familiar with *warm* colors (reds, oranges, yellows) and *cool* colors (blues, greens, purples). These are generalities, however. It is possible to have a quite cool red or a very warm green. The important thing to remember in regard to emphasis and subordination is that when we place a warm object amidst a sea of cool objects, that warm object really pops to the eye. The reverse is true as well, but usually not to the same degree.

COLOR SATURATION. *Saturation* refers to how pure and intense a color is. Imagine the brightest, purest, most intense red that you can imagine. That would be saturated. Now imagine a red that is quite gray and much less intense, as if one took gray paint and added just a bit of pink or burgundy paint to it. We refer to grayed colors as *desaturated* colors. Objects in saturated colors will stand out more than objects in desaturated colors. A flaming red sun on the horizon is an obvious focal point to a sunset scene.

We use the above tools to add emphasis, and we back off in the use of a tool to indicate subordination. Several of the tools should be used in combination; use of only one tool is usually not effective enough. Thus, if I want the hearth to be the focal point in a room, I may use the following tools: *size*—I make sure that it is the largest object in the room; *lighting*—I purposefully place accent lighting over the fireplace; *context*—the brick texture is the strongest texture in the room; and *color saturation*—when a fire is burning, the fire displays the warmest and most saturated color of the entire room. If I determine that a neighboring wall should be subordinate, I use less contrast than on the hearth wall (smaller-sized objects, less direct lighting, less textural contrast, less color temperature and saturation variation, etc.).

The main focal point is sometimes the easiest part of the hierarchy to create. Purposefully subordinating other areas often demands more careful thought. I usually approach a room by determining which wall or area of the room will be the main focal point for the entire room, then I approach each wall as a *sub*composition, making sure that it displays its own hierarchy while adding to the overall room hierarchy. This may sound complicated or difficult, but it gets easier with practice.

The nice thing about room decor is that changes and experimentation are relatively easy, involving at most the repainting of a wall, but more often much easier fixes such as moving a piece of furniture or rearranging items on a table. As you experiment with the principles of emphasis and subordination you'll find that they are some of the most powerful principles to effectuate incredible interior designs.

Dining Rooms

Dining rooms are another part of the Early American country home that can be really fun to create. While there are certain things that kitchens or bathrooms need to have in order to be kitchens or bathrooms, there are less rules to follow in a dining room. There obviously needs to be a table and some chairs, but outside of that the sky is the limit. You can give a dining room whatever feel you want. Some folks prefer a very formal setting; others prefer an extremely casual setting. Either is appropriate, as well as a mix of the two.

The dining area can be combined with the kitchen, or with a family or keeping room. Once again, a hearth is tough to beat in creating a homey, comfortable dining area. Some homeowners create one specifically for the dining room; others borrow the light, warmth, and ambiance from the neighboring kitchen or keeping room hearth. As always, building elements such as hewn beams and wooden floors, primitive painted antique or reproduction furnishings and lighting, and casual, knobby textures in rock, stone, rag rugs, place mats, or napkins help impart the warm, cozy atmosphere that we all enjoy in a dining area.

One of my favorite treatments in dining rooms is mixing and mismatching (using the principle of repetition with variation). One can get away with this much more in an Early

American country interior. For example, who says all the chairs have to match? A smattering of different kinds and styles can be a whimsical treat for the eye. The chairs

don't all have to be from the same period, but there should be at least a little bit of thought behind the scheme. Make it obvious that they're *supposed* to be mismatched. For instance, one would be better off to pair two ladder-backs with two Windsors, rather than try to find close matches to the original two Windsors. Another possible approach would be to have a set of Windsors, but with none of them obviously matching.

Dining rooms in many old homesteads appeared quite primitive at first glance, with rough-hewn log walls, hand-built furniture, and wooden puncheon floors. But many proudly displayed, for instance, an inherited set of fine china. While treenware, pottery, pewter, or enamelware might have been the everyday choice for meals, the china was used for special occasions—to show that the frontier wife wasn't completely coarse or unrefined. Any of the everyday choices still make excellent serving objects, but modern reproductions are a wiser choice to actually serve and eat from (antique pewter often contained lead, as did glazes on old pottery).

Dining tables are another great place for creativity. Old sawbuck or farmhouse tables are a joy to behold in and of themselves. There are several furniture builders across the country that build quality reproduction tables and chairs with an old-style character but new, modern usability and comfort. Be patient and thoughtful and you'll have a dining area that will be a treat for the eyes. Create a warm, comfortable, friendly gathering place for your family, and meals there will be special, pleasurable, inviting occasions rather than just another refueling stop.

Elements such as old colonial fireplaces and cage bars add
a special Early American ambiance to any dining room.

There are so many items that are "just right" in these two
dining rooms. I'll let the reader explore and find all of them.

While restoring this dining room in the Libbey Home, original
paint revealed that a cabinet had been along the large wall,
so David T. Smith built a new one matching the old marks.

*John and Jill Mahan's
new home in Kentucky is a
wonderful combination of old
accents in a new floor plan,
as this dining room open
to the family room shows.*

Dining Rooms

The dining room should,
above all, be a place
that family can relax
and enjoy one another's
company and a bountiful
life. Early American style
does this like no other.

BALANCE

Balance is, and always will be, one of the most important principles of design. There are two types of balance: the first deals with *visual weight;* the second refers to an overall *balance of elements*—in other words, not too many or too few of any particular element.

Visual Weight

Every item in a composition has a *weight,* or in other words commands a certain amount of *visual attention*. Large things usually command attention, as do high-contrast items. This may sound like we're repeating the principles of emphasis and subordination again—and it is closely related. However, it is possible to create a composition that perfectly emphasizes and subordinates but is horrible in regard to balance.

The easiest way to understand balance is to first consider *symmetrical* balance, which is when a composition displays an exact mirror image on both sides of a central axis (either vertical or horizontal). Early American architecture shows this type of balance very frequently, as it was considered ideal in classical, Renaissance, and colonial times.

Closely related to perfect symmetry is *near symmetry*. This is when the two halves have nearly identical visual weight on both sides of the axis, yet are not perfect mirror images.

Asymmetrical compositions display different visual weights on the two sides of the axis. For example, picture a 50-pound boy on a seesaw trying to balance with his 200-pound father on the other end. The boy will never be able to balance with his dad as long as they are the same distance from the *fulcrum*, the central support of the seesaw. In order for the two to balance, the young boy needs more *leverage*. He can gain this by sliding out toward the end as far as possible and having Dad slide toward the fulcrum. At a certain point the two will balance. Remember this analogy when balancing asymmetrical compositions. After determining where your axis is, move large object(s) slightly closer to the axis and small object(s) a bit closer to the edge of the composition to achieve balance of visual weight.

Balance of Elements

Let's suppose you have a relatively neutral color palette in a room, and you decide to create a focal point in a room with a bright red place setting on a table. First of all, you're thinking in the right direction by creating emphasis and subordination! However, if that place setting is the only red in the entire room, there will be a feeling of imbalance because the red is such an anomaly. It's important to add hints or splashes of red in a few more parts of the room to achieve a visual balance.

An artist friend of mine often says, "If it looks wrong—add more of it." Often the first brushstroke of a bright color on a painting, such as a saturated yellow, often looks wrong because it is the only place on the painting with that color. As one continues to add more of that yellow to the composition, that initial brushstroke starts to feel like it belongs. The same is true with colors (or textures or other elements) in an interior composition. Keep adding until about 30 percent of the room includes that particular color, texture, or other element. (The significance of that 30 percent will be discussed in later sections.)

Pantries, Butteries, and Washrooms

Few things are as historically charming as a well-stocked, old-fashioned pantry. (And few things are as *un*charming as a modern pantry.) Pantries evoke a tremendous sense of self-reliance and preparedness when thoughtfully and meticulously well stocked. Brimming with the homemade products of the farm, they represent the embodiment of a simpler life. Folks in the past knew and valued self-reliance, recognized the importance of providing for one's family, and worked hard throughout the seasons to be able to enjoy, literally, the fruits of their labors. We have lost much of that frame of mind in our modern world. It would do us well to regain it. A pantry in the home is a good place to start.

The visual spaces of Early American homes give me a tangible connection to the simplicity of life. But I would rather see a well-thought-out, prepared-for-the-worst pantry than a visually pleasing one. However, because that wouldn't add to the ambiance of the home, I wouldn't necessarily put that kind of stocked pantry on display. Some owners of Early American homes have two different pantry spaces—a modern one and a historical one. Some combine the two spaces, keeping modern goods behind closed cabinet doors and historical things out in the open. Either approach is great, but my preference is the second.

To have a well-stocked pantry that also looks authentic is an admirable thing. There are so many wonderful old containers that are just begging to be more than just objects of art, that long to be useful again. And few things are as gratifying to see as row upon row of newly canned jars of vegetables or colorful preserves. If using new jars, just cover the lids with kraft paper or old-timey fabric tied on with jute twine. That way you can place them on open shelves rather than behind closed doors. This look may not be as primitive as some would choose, but nevertheless adds to the country farmhouse atmosphere.

Although I have been involved with the restoration of old homes for about 25 years, I am still wet behind the ears compared to my friend Ginny Curry. Ginny has amassed a wealth of knowledge and expertise through many years of observing, creating, and dealing in Early American objects and spaces. Following are some of Ginny's thoughts about primitive, more authentic pantries.

Designing Authentic Early American Pantries

In New England these storage areas were called "butteries," but in the rest of the states they were referred to as "pantries." No matter how much space you have or don't have, a pantry/buttery is a must, and so fun to incorporate into your home. When confronted with little space, we have taken a hall closet and made it into a pantry by just taking the door off and covering all surfaces with old wood. Add barnwood or painted-board shelving, and voila!—you are ready to go.

Early pantries housed pantry boxes, barrels, wooden bowls, apothecaries, and crocks. Just like then, they are still a great place to store food items. Dried beans, corn, sunflowers, and gourds are always a must, and to add to the look, display them in the open. Don't forget to hang an apron or linen towel on a nail.

If you are able to construct a larger pantry, which is mostly shelving, try jutting the lower shelves out a few inches further than the top ones and you can use this area as a buffet shelf for parties and holidays. Most of our pantries have all walls, ceilings, and other surfaces covered in old wood, along with the shelving. Incorporating a small cupboard at one end of the pantry is always good if you have the space.

*Antique items like a
butter churn (left)
or original pantry
boxes (overleaf) can
add such a nice flavor
to pantries, kitchens,
and dining rooms.*

Along with pantries, laundry facilities can be a great space to display rather than to hide—if one is creative.

Pantries and washrooms can even share a
common space. Early American folk were an
ingenious lot; why shouldn't we be?

Many early porches have been closed off after decades and even centuries of use. This sink in a West Virginia cottage sits in a porch-turned-laundry room.

Ginny Curry cuts the shelf supports back to create a serving buffet, like this one in friend Pat Linton's pantry.

*Forgotten corners of an
entry or mudroom can be
greatly enhanced by adding
Early American styling.*

Pantries, Butteries, and Washrooms 95

Some pantries are completely usable, others have display areas with modern packages hidden behind old doors. You get to choose!

Overleaf: Even small nooks can be enhanced by creating a miniature pantry, like this converted window in a stone wall.

THE RULE OF THREE *and*
THE GOLDEN SECTION

The *rule of three* is one of the most used principles of design. It is quite simple but very effective. By a stroke of good fortune, the rule of three happens to have three parts.

The first part involves *dividing a space into three equal parts,* either horizontally or vertically, or both. Doing so enables one to then position objects either in these divided spaces or along one of the dividing lines, and know that the placement will be pleasing to the human eye.

I'm often asked how high a wainscot (an area of wooden paneling on the lower part of a wall) should be. The answer is however high you want it—but using the rule of three guarantees that it will be visually appealing. If you have a standard eight-foot wall (96 inches), a wainscot that is 32 inches high (one-third of 96 inches) will look good. This will divide the wall into two sections that follow a ratio of one-third to two-thirds, or 1:2. If I were to vary the height, or add a trim piece to the top, I would make it taller rather than shorter, to move the design toward the golden section ratio (see below). The same goes for determining the appropriate height for a chair rail.

Here's another example. Let's say you're arranging furniture against a wall. You could take a traditional symmetrical approach, centering the couch on the wall, hanging a painting centered above it, adding an end table on each side of the couch, placing matching lamps on the end tables, and so on, to create a very formal look. But let's say that rather than the formal look you'd like something slightly less confined; or maybe you happen to have a step-back cupboard instead of end tables. Picture an imaginary vertical line running from top to bottom, two-thirds of the way along that same wall. Position the couch and painting in the larger two-thirds section, and the step-back cupboard in the remaining one-third section. Make sure to have an element or two that overlap that imaginary line to tie the composition together. This part of the rule of three ties in closely with asymmetrical balance (see the principle of balance in the previous chapter).

Part two of the rule of three involves *arranging objects into groups of three*. You'll see this in countless classical designs: a grouping of three windows; a wall with three arches; a central structure with two symmetrical wings. Use this principle everywhere: three pillows on a bed; three baskets on a shelf; three stockings on a mantle. If three are too few, try five or seven. As a general rule, odd numbers feel more casual while even numbers lend an air of formality. Don't forget what you've learned about repetition with variation. Try a big, a medium, and a small pantry box in a stack; a large central cupboard with two smaller flanking cupboards; or three equally sized old decoys of different colors or species.

Part three of the rule of three has to do with *scale*. How does one know if a composition is too sparse or too busy? I usually begin by filling approximately two-thirds of the space and leaving about one-third of "negative space." This is not a hard-and-fast rule, but is a great place to start. So if I were arranging the couch, painting, and step-back cupboard above, I would add additional objects, such as lamps, baskets, smaller paintings, or an old gameboard, until those objects ("positive shapes") filled up about two-thirds of the total wall space and the negative space around the objects comprised about one-third of the space. That usually looks about right—but feel free to take away something or add something according to what feels right to you.

An alternative to using the rule of three is to use a similar ratio known as the *golden section*, or golden mean. The golden section is a ratio of 1 to 1.618—or in easier-to-use figures, a ratio of about 5:8. So instead of arranging a composition so that it's divided into three equal spaces in a ratio of 1:2, the golden section suggests that we divide a composition into *thirteen* equal spaces, then divide those spaces into two sections (one of five spaces and one of eight spaces), thus yielding a ratio of 5:8. Many designers find this ratio to be more aesthetically pleasing than the rule of three.

The golden section can also be used for other types of space divisions. For example, a room that measures 10 feet by 16 feet (a ratio of 5:8) will just feel *right* as a rectangle—not too narrow or too stubby. Wall and ceiling height will obviously play a part in this example, but the main idea is that this ratio is a pleasing one to the human brain. It is a ratio I often turn to when solving architectural or interior design issues.

Bedrooms

The thing I like most about bedrooms in Early American country homes is that they have the capacity to be the most historically correct spaces. Everywhere else, concessions must be made for modern living. Kitchens need refrigerators and bathrooms need toilets, but bedrooms, for the most part, have retained the same uses and furnishings for well over two hundred years. The biggest exception to this is, of course, electricity. But it is relatively easy to tuck an outlet or power cord behind a dresser, chair, or basket. And fortunately there are many makers and sellers of excellent reproduction lighting fixtures. Although most major lighting manufacturers now have product lines that hint toward a historical look, the smaller independent makers do such wonderful work that it's a shame to go to the trouble of restoring or creating a historically styled structure and not take advantage of their works.

The other most notable detour from historical accuracy in a bedroom is the fact that modern bedding is far more comfortable than anything they had back then. Obviously the mattress gets covered up, so this isn't a visual issue. We have one of the newfangled adjustable air mattresses, yet most folks wouldn't know it without seeing the controls tucked under pillows. And our oldest daughter uses an adjustable hospital-type bed because of a disability. We were able to find a great reproduction bed without too much trouble that more or less wraps around her bed frame and, combined with a bit of creative bed skirting, hides the modern necessities completely. We have some old quilts that we display on the beds, but to preserve these we have reproduction quilts and blankets that we use most often.

Ginny Curry uses (and sells) wonderful bed coverings that have the appearance of old-time straw or feather ticks. They bulge up like a freshly baked loaf of bread and look absolutely wonderful. Reproduction bed frames, crafted by historically minded furniture makers, are also relatively easy to find. And antique beds are often still in usable shape. They often don't match modern mattress sizes, but that issue is not insurmountable. Some folks have new side rails made in a modern size that function like the antique ones— so that the originals are preserved (but not used). In the case of relatively inexpensive iron beds, we have several times cut the rails in two and welded in extensions. The mattresses sometimes are a bit wider than old headboards and footboards, but not enough to be noticeably distracting.

The remainder of the bedroom is quite easily decorated in Early American style. Old bedrooms were often quite sparse, so one needn't get too elaborate. One or two dressers, actual antiques or carefully created reproductions, work just as well now as they did then. Generally, built-in closets are rare in older homes, but armoires are a wonderful alternative. If you have the great fortune of having an old home with built-in closets, or are creating a new home with a historical personality, antique closet doors can add to the ambiance. Find old doors that work, or find a creative, historically minded craftsman to make some. The Shakers were masters at storage, and a close study of their built-ins can yield ideas for incredibly practical modern cabinetry.

Generally speaking, I love a period look but am more concerned about comfort and practicality than 100 percent authenticity. There are some homeowners, however, who pick a date—say 1775, because of the history of their home—and then have to have every item be pre-1775. I am involved in historical reenactment groups, and we are meticulous

about that sort of thing in our dress and accoutrements, so I understand and admire the homeowner who attains a goal like that. But really anywhere on the authenticity spectrum is right, as long as it's what you want. By not being too concerned with 100 percent authenticity, we also have license to be creative and have fun—sometimes using items that folks probably wouldn't have used 100 years ago in a bedroom. For instance, we might keep our socks in pantry boxes, use a grain bin salvaged from the barn for a dirty clothes hamper, or store sweaters in an antique pie safe. We love the look, so it works for us. As with most areas of a historical home, creativity always trumps expensiveness. Impress your friends with your inventiveness and originality rather than price tags.

Bedrooms can be embellished with just the amount of Early
American styling that is right for you—there are no rules.

Two bedrooms in Virginia masterfully built by Noah H. Bradley III and artfully decorated by Marise Craig.

Some of the loveliest Early American bedrooms
that I have seen have been children's bedrooms.

Early American styling in the Tucker House—a
Louisville, Kentucky, bed-and-breakfast—helps one
truly escape the hustle and bustle of modern life.

Again, there are no rules about decorating in Early American style. Choose how little or how much you want.

Noah H. Bradley III often exposes the original beams of a home. In this case, atmosphere trumps authenticity for a sensational look.

I often wonder if our
forefathers (and mothers)
would have loved the
feeling of modern carpet
underfoot! As you can see,
one can easily incorporate
this new material into an
Early American setting.

Two views of David T. and Lora Smith's master bedroom. Lora designs some of the most cozy interiors that I have ever had the great fortune to see and photograph. One has to ask, "How do you leave this every morning?"

ALIGNMENT

One of the principles of design most used in classical, Georgian, and Federal-style architecture is that of *alignment.* Sadly, in recent years fewer people are aware of its importance as a visual principle. Alignment simply refers to lining things up, where the tops or bottoms of objects (or both) fall on the same imaginary horizontal line, or the sides of objects align vertically. One of the most common examples of this can be found in the window configuration of many period homes. Unfortunately, many modern residences have window configurations and sizes that perhaps are logical when inside the home, but make virtually no sense on the exterior of the home.

Alignment occurs in well-designed homes in many more ways than just windows on the vertical plane of a wall. Countless old homes were built on a perfectly symmetrical axis through the center of the house, with a front door that opens to a central hall and a back door directly through the hall, aligned with the front door. Many of these homes have another axis centered from end to end, directly under the peak of the roof—especially those with fireplaces on both ends. Generally these types of homes have floor plans that are almost a mirror image from one side to the other. Usually they have been added onto over time, so the symmetry may not continue through the entire house (which is fine—remember the principle of repetition with variation).

Alignment can occur in many other forms as well, such as a doorway directly across the room from a fireplace or a window directly under the peak of a roof. If you live in a home that exhibits this type of architecture you are fortunate—take advantage of it.

The principle of alignment should be utilized as one furnishes and decorates the interior as well, for it always conveys a feeling that every item rests exactly where it belongs. Alignment will usually lend a formal look to any space, so you probably won't want to overdo it (again, use the idea of repetition with variation). I seldom find homes where alignment is possible in too many places, so I generally take advantage of it whenever the opportunity presents itself.

Most folks inherently know about aligning a dining room table directly under a light fixture, aligning a table directly in front of a window, or aligning a bed directly under the peak of a pitched ceiling. But here are a few other opportunities to use alignment that you might not have considered. If you have a blank wall directly across the room from a doorway, consider aligning a painting or a cupboard with the doorway, and building the composition of the wall around that painting or cupboard. By incorporating light into that composition at the focal point of the painting or cupboard (say a picture light above the painting, or a lamp on the cupboard), one creates an experience that Sarah Susanka refers to as "light to walk toward" in her excellent book *Home by Design*. Doing so has the special effect of warmly inviting one into the room, and adds that much more coziness to the home.

Aligning any object, or group of objects, with the top of a window creates a sense that they "belong" to the wall. If you have a window above your kitchen sink, consider placing a focal point, aligned with the window, out in the yard. A picturesque garden shed, an old goat cart, or a bed of flowers will be especially attractive if it appears in just the right spot in your exterior landscape. Few concepts are as effective as the use of alignment to create a sense of every item being in its proper place.

Bathrooms

In the Early American home, bathrooms, like kitchens, can pose interesting challenges. Obviously original Early American homes didn't even have indoor bathrooms, so creating a 100 percent authentic bathroom is an impossibility (unless you opt for an outhouse!). However, bathrooms can actually be one of the most creative spaces in your home, with a surprisingly authentic feel to them. The key is to simply have fun.

Bathrooms are a great place to present the unexpected. Strive to impress with creativity rather than high price tags. Here are just a few examples:

- We used antique galvanized, corrugated roofing—salvaged from an old barn—for a tub surround in one of our homes.

- David T. Smith often insets a galvanized or copper washtub or bucket into a bathroom countertop. He has them plumbed for use as a sink.

- Reclaimed (or new) claw-foot tubs always lend a fun old atmosphere. Although most folks recognize that they're from 1940 instead of 1840, most also have an innate understanding and forgiveness for the historical latitude. Same goes for modern toilets.

- Antique-styled beaded paneling is especially appropriate in bathrooms. So are Shaker pegboards.

- One of my favorite bathroom counter treatments is aged copper or tin—it can be bent over the edges of the surface and tacked with rusty nails.

- Bathrooms are perfect places for the odd container. Don't go out and buy toothbrush, toilet paper, or shampoo holders from a retail store—find something unusual and funky at a flea market or antique store, or even in Granddad's barn.

- I recently visited a home where the owners had created an outhouse just off a family room. They took a modern toilet and built a structure around it with old barnwood, complete with a cover over the seat. Everything

was true to form except for the modern usability and convenience. Code required that there be a sink, so just outside the outhouse was an old wooden barrel with a galvanized tub inset into the top—plumbed, of course, as a sink.

Ginny Curry is the master
at creating primitive styling,
as in these two bathrooms
in her home. I love the ideas
that she comes up with!

Early American styling does not have to be primitive in look or comfort.
Some of the most lavish bathrooms I have seen have been done in this
style. They can truly be a place to unwind and wash all cares away!

Occasionally David T. Smith crafts handmade copper sinks to add to the Early American styling in bathrooms, kitchens, and laundry rooms.

Bathrooms should be places that are inviting and cozy spaces.
Modern, slick surfaces don't say that—to me, anyway!

HARMONY

The principle of *harmony* is at least partly achieved by effectively using all the other design principles we've covered. However, one could be effective in applying all the other principles but still not achieve harmony—in the same way that harmony in music requires all the notes to work perfectly together as well as on their own. For example, let's suppose that one were to create a composition that exhibited repetition with variation, a great focal point, perfect asymmetrical balance, and correct alignment. The whole design could be thrown out of whack by using objects, materials, or colors that are completely out of harmony with each other. One must be conscious of the other principles of design, and must also be certain that they are all working well together.

While I certainly support eclectic decorating, there are combinations that simply don't make sense. As I often share with my college students, "everything doesn't go with everything." Fortunately, every Early American element naturally exudes a historical aura, and additionally the materials, textures, and colors have a tendency to harmonize together. This is one reason that Early American country interiors are so visually appealing. Few other modes of decorating are so coherent, so harmonious.

An easy way for an artist to guarantee having a harmony of colors is to limit the palette of colors to choose from. Historical manufacturing processes and materials were more limited than our modern ones, so decorating with historical items automatically limits our palette of materials, textures, and colors. In decorating an Early American country home, there are still hundreds of choices, but the limiting factors work to our advantage. These historical limitations create a harmony that few modern homes demonstrate. We'll explore those materials, textures, and colors a bit more in the next chapter.

What if one wants a more eclectic look and doesn't care about 100 percent authenticity? If you want a basically modern home with a few touches of historical or primitive furnishings sprinkled in, be aware that any variations to your modern decorations will appear unplanned until you have *enough* of them. In one of our previous homes, for example, we had a bit of an "Early American farmhouse meets old sporting lodge" look. Scattered amongst the primitive cupboards, Windsor chairs, and shaker boxes sat the occasional timeworn decoy, a pair of vintage wooden skis, and an old canvas canoe hanging from the ceiling. The difference in these two styles wasn't too wide, and we made certain that there was enough variation.

I usually apply the rule of three when choosing how much variation to add to a look to maintain harmony. Whether adding a historical look to a modern home or adding an eclectic look to a historical home, harmony is usually achieved when the variation approaches 30 percent of the total. This is not a hard and fast rule, but it's a helpful place to begin.

Other Spaces

We've covered most of the main areas in a home, but there are a few other spaces that may or may not be in your historical restoration or reproduction home that still deserve at least a bit of attention. While traveling the country to photograph the remarkable homes in this book, I have enjoyed finding many of these "miscellaneous" spaces, of which I've included a few samples here for your enjoyment.

Many homes have entries, side rooms, TV rooms, stairways . . . the list of spaces that don't fall into any of the previously mentioned categories goes on and on. Each of these areas is a great place to have fun and be creative. Again, the only rules that apply are the rules of visual design that you have been learning about in the sidebars of this book.

As I write this, we are just beginning another home restoration. This home was originally built around 1890, but its style is from a simpler time—more like a home from the mid-nineteenth century—and it did not originally have a laundry room. The existing one began life elsewhere as a chicken coop, and is now part of an enclosed back porch connected to the kitchen. Early American homes are quirky this way—but it is part of what I love about them.

Stairways can be one of the most sensational parts of a restored or re-created historical home. I have seen them range from extremely rustic—built from old hand-hewn beams—to very refined, and everywhere in between. They are great places to get creative with design, paint, craftsmanship, etc.

Porches are one thing that early Americans had mastered. Though some modern homes have them, they're never quite the same as the old ones. Some old ones were small but quaint, and some were large and stately. Regardless of size, antique porches have character that is difficult to capture today. If you're faced with constructing a new reproduction home, study old porches very carefully. Don't try to improve upon old ones—it can't be done. If you have an old porch, consider yourself blessed. They are like venerable friends—always there, always welcoming.

Lothar Janke reconstructed
these stairs in his restored
stone home in central Utah.
A craftsman originally
from East Germany, his
work is much like that of the
original European settlers
who built this home.

Don't be afraid to use
Early American items
for uses other than those
intended, like quilts as art,
or a kitchen cupboard to store
clothing in the bedroom.

We have the great fortune
of having more leisure
time than most of our
ancestors. These leisure
spaces can be decorated in
Early American style too.

Unusual textures can make a huge difference in a home. Builder Noah H. Bradley III often combines hewn beams, stone, sawn and painted lumber, smooth wooden floors, and plastered walls to vary the textures from room to room.

MATERIALS, TEXTURES,
and COLORS

As I design architectural exteriors or interiors, there are two main questions that I continually ask myself regarding *materials, textures,* and *colors.* First, "Is there something old that I could use here rather than something new?" Second, as was best expressed by G. Lawson Drinkard III in his wonderful book *Old Wood/New Home,* "As you contemplate each planning decision, ask yourself, 'What can I do here that will make my heart sing?'"

Normally when confronted with a furnishing need in the home, the first inclination is to run down to the local furniture store and pick up something affordable. When designing in Early American style, this approach should be the *last* resort. That doesn't mean it should be avoided altogether, but consider the options below first.

Is there something old that was originally used for the function in mind that would work just as well now? This may be the case with something like an old cupboard. There are few things that a new cupboard does better than an old one. The door may sag a bit or one leg may need to be slightly propped up, but usually those little quirks just add to the charm. On occasion an old cupboard can be in such bad shape that continual opening and closing of doors actually damages the cupboard, in which case one may wish to use the cupboard only for things that are accessed rarely.

Or is there something old that *wasn't* necessarily used for this function, but would be a creative alternative? My wife, Johnna, is especially inventive in this area. Who says pencils on a desk can't be stored in a saltware crock rather than a drawer? Is there something the same basic size as an end table that could act as one? One of my favorite pieces of furniture that I came across while photographing this book was not a piece of furniture at all—it was an old grain bin salvaged from an aged barn, used as a display table in John and Jill Mahan's home.

If something old doesn't foot the bill, is there a reasonable new alternative that won't take away from the atmosphere? In some instances old items are undesirable. Certain plumbing and electrical needs are best handled with new items. New appliances are usually better than old ones. Many new furnishings are more pest-proof than antique examples. Sometimes one is much more concerned with comfort than exact historical correctness. Our couches and chairs are often new items, but selected with a historical look in mind. Items can be found at furniture stores, unfinished furniture outlets, or big-box stores that, with a coat of a period paint color and some careful distressing, will fit well into the big picture. Be wary of cheap, mass-produced items that attempt to copy the Early American country look but only result in compromising authenticity and believability. Stick with real items as much as possible, which might take a bit more searching to find, but in the end will be much more visually satisfying.

Many items in Early American decorating and construction don't have to be of the highest professional quality. After all, many items in early America were created in the farmyard woodshed. Whenever possible and viable, reusing old materials such as wood, stone, and metals such as old-style tin and copper adds authenticity and has the added benefits of thrift and the responsible stewardship of resources.

Pay close attention to examples of historical styles and methods of manufacture. One of the biggest mistakes of modern builders of structures and furnishings revolves around scale. A good example of this is the size of standard door and window trim found in most stores today. Generally speaking, they are too small in proportion to the areas they trim. In historical buildings, larger trim was often used. That doesn't mean that new trim can't be used, but one may need to build up several layers of it to avoid the pitfalls of incorrect scale.

Have you ever walked into a newly completed home to find the same exact *texture* over every square inch of drywall, the same trim around every door and window, and the same floor covering in every room? As was discussed previously in the section on repetition with variation, too much of anything becomes wearisome—including textures. Texture is perhaps the design element least understood by the layperson. The key is to change it up. It's okay to have drywall, but look for a few places where you can offer variation—a wood-paneled wall or wainscot, or a stone or brick hearth. Then add that variation in at least three places. I love how hewn beams break up large expanses of drywall. Antique materials will often offer the needed changes in texture. That is another reason why Early American style is inherently visually appealing: the textures are appropriately repetitive while also providing variation. Given a choice of fabrics or materials, don't be afraid to choose rougher, knobbier textures as you layer different furnishings, objects, and components into your architecture or interiors.

There are no hard-and-fast rules concerning which *colors* you have to use—it's your home. But limiting your palette to traditional colors will simplify your efforts and enable you to achieve the important harmony discussed previously. I am more concerned with creating a historical atmosphere than I am with exact authenticity. Even though many historical colors were actually much brighter—even somewhat glaring—than what we normally think of, there are certain colors that we tend to associate with Early American style. There are several companies that specialize in historical paint colors. My suggestion is to choose a handful of colors—five or six at most—that appeal to you, and use them scattered throughout every room in your home in painted trim, furnishings, and fabrics. An occasional variation from the palette won't hurt—just don't get too carried away. The ideal is to arrive at the sweet spot between variety and unity.

Exterior Spaces

Yes, I'm well aware this book is entitled *Early American Country Interiors*. I'm also aware that *exterior* spaces are not normally considered interiors. But if you've made it this far through the book, you are probably interested in historical structures enough that you wouldn't mind seeing what the outsides of some of these homes look like. Personally, I love the outsides every bit as much as the insides. I'm guessing most of you do as well. So before we wrap things up and put a bow on, please allow me to share some of them.

If you've read the sidebars in this book, you are now hopefully more aware of the use of design principles in Early American architecture and decorating, something that will help you understand more about Early American homes. Early American homes used these principles as much on the outside as they did the inside—perhaps even more so, for the exterior was the most public face of the building. See if you can spot examples of the uses of repetition with variation, focal points, balance, the rule of three, alignment, and harmony in the photos that follow—sort of our own little historical version of "Where's Waldo?"

I absolutely love all of the varieties of materials,
textures, and colors available for those of
us who enjoy Early American style.

Two views of Dan and Janet Edwards' colonial home in Michigan. Gardens can be as formal or casual as one chooses.

Early American style affords the hanging of flags more than any other style. Sometimes the home seems almost incomplete without one!

Left: JoAnne Erdman's Hydrangea Hill in Ohio is based on several old colonial homes of New England.

Sara Jense restored an ancestral home in central Utah. She, too, was highly influenced by colonial homes of New England, where she had traveled countless times.

*Early American styling
has just enough formality
to feel classic and right,
yet just enough casualness
to feel cozy as well.*

It is my hope that you have enjoyed your visit to these wonderful homes as much as I have. Farewell and God bless!